This project was supported by Grant Number 2010-CK-WX-K001 awarded by the Office of Community Oriented Policing Services, U.S. Department of Justice. The opinions contained herein are those of the author(s) and do not necessarily represent the official position or policies of the U.S. Department of Justice. References to specific agencies, companies, products, or services should not be considered an endorsement by the author(s) or the U.S. Department of Justice. Rather, the references are illustrations to supplement discussion of the issues.

The Internet references cited in this publication were valid as of the date of this publication. Given that URLs and websites are in constant flux, neither the author nor the COPS Office can vouch for their current validity.

March 2011

2011

ELECTRONIC CONTROL WEAPON GUIDELINES

Table of Contents

Letter from the Director 2

Foreword 3

Acknowledgments 5

Introduction 8

Guiding Principles for ECWs 10

Electronic Control Weapon Guidelines 17

Background Information 25

References 39

Glossary 41

Appendix A: PERF Executive Session Participants 44

Appendix B: Working Group Participants 50

About the COPS Office 52

About PERF 53

Letter from the Director

Dear Colleagues,

In partnership with the Police Executive Research Forum (PERF), I am pleased to present the *2011 Electronic Control Weapon Guidelines*—the result of a national survey that examined the use of ECWs, specifically what policies, practices, and training were being employed in the field. The knowledge gained from this research helped frame the discussions that took place during a two-day meeting and workshop, organized by the COPS Office and PERF, to discuss the issues surrounding ECWs with a combination of police, doctors, attorneys, researchers, and other experts.

These guidelines embody the knowledge and consensus of the key stakeholders present at the meeting and represent the public's best interest in regards to safety. The COPS Office and PERF facilitated an honest discussion between experts of key fields by acting as an independent arbiter on a difficult issue.

I want to emphasize that no weapon is a substitute for effective police work, and no weapon should be incorporated into the range of force options available to the police at the expense of diminishing the fundamental skills of communicating with subjects and de-escalating tense encounters. Nonetheless, the information and guidelines presented here should assist in ensuring this force technology is used in the most appropriate and effective manner possible.

I hope you will find this publication helpful in your local efforts, and we encourage you to share this publication, as well as your successes, with other law enforcement practitioners.

Sincerely,

Bernard K. Melekian
Director
Office of Community Oriented Policing Services
U.S. Department of Justice

Foreword

One of the defining characteristics of police organizations is that they have been given legal authority to use physical force, and one of the most critical challenges for police departments is the constant struggle to ensure that their use of force is legitimate. Over the last few decades, there has been a growing awareness that police must strive not only to prevent unnecessary or excessive uses of force but also to ensure that communities perceive their police to be acting properly when they use force.

As a result of this greater attention to use-of-force issues, there have been substantial improvements in policies, practices, and results. These include significant reductions in officer-involved shootings, creation of early intervention systems to detect possible excesses in individual officers' use of force, greater mechanisms for accountability and transparency regarding use-of-force issues, and training of officers to de-escalate situations when possible using verbal techniques and other nonlethal methods of controlling an incident.

Another advancement has been the development of new less-lethal weapons, which give police a wider range of options to choose from in dealing with persons who resist police authority in various situations—in some cases because they have a mental illness or are under the influence of drugs. Each new less-lethal weapon brings its own set of advantages and limitations that must be managed if officers are to choose the best options in a given situation.

In 2005, the COPS Office and PERF came together to produce a set of policy guidelines regarding the use of what were then called Conducted Energy Devices and now are called Electronic Control Weapons (ECWs). Police practitioners and other experts met in Houston and were able to hammer out a strong set of guidelines on ECW use. The guidelines offered practical guidance on the situations in which ECWs are useful and those in which they are not the best option, as well as advice about best practices for training, supervision of officers' ECW activations, and other issues. The COPS/PERF guidelines of 2005 were adopted by many departments, and they helped those agencies to ensure that ECWs were used properly.

Since 2005, researchers have continued to conduct studies of ECWs, and thousands of police departments have gained real-world experience with them. As a result, the COPS Office asked PERF to update the 2005 guidelines, reflecting these developments. PERF conducted background research, including a survey of nearly 200 law enforcement agencies regarding ECW deployments, as well as interviews of police chiefs and other experts. PERF and the COPS Office then convened a conference in Philadelphia in August 2010 where 150 police executives, researchers, doctors, attorneys, and others discussed the use of ECWs in light of five years' worth of experience in the field.

This publication is the result of those efforts, providing an updated and improved version of the initial guidelines to reflect the state of the field regarding ECWs. The 2011 guidelines also reflect a general consensus in policing that ECWs play an invaluable role in providing officers with another type of less-lethal weapon that can be effective in many situations, but they should not be seen as an all-purpose weapon that takes the place of de-escalation techniques and other options. In addition, ECWs have limitations, so officers must be prepared to switch to other strategies if an ECW is not producing the desired result.

We hope that law enforcement agencies will find these new guidelines helpful as they work to continue the advances that progressive police agencies have made in the responsible and humane use of force.

Bernard K. Melekian
Director
Office of Community Oriented Policing Services
U.S. Department of Justice

Chuck Wexler
Executive Director
Police Executive Research Forum

Acknowledgments

We would like to thank the COPS Office for providing us with the opportunity to re-examine this significant law enforcement issue. The use of Electronic Control Weapons (ECWs) by law enforcement agencies in this country has grown substantially. With this increased use has come more insight into when and how the weapons are most effective. At the same time, the courts have weighed in on what constitutes appropriate use. Our knowledge about the weapons has increased, and with that knowledge came the realization that the set of Conducted Energy Device (CED) guidelines developed in 2005 needed to be updated.

We would like to offer our thanks to Bernard Melekian, director of the COPS Office, for recognizing the importance of updating the ECW guidelines. Mora Fiedler, our program manager, was enthusiastic and helpful as we planned the various components of this project.

We thank those police chiefs and other professionals who were able to join us for the Guidelines for Policy and Practice Executive Session held in Philadelphia, August 2010 (see Appendix A for a list of all attendees). We want to recognize and thank Chuck Ramsey, police commissioner of Philadelphia, who hosted the meeting and worked with us to identify many of the key issues for the meeting's agenda.

We would particularly like to thank the following presenters: Dr. Alex Eastman, M.D., who shared his expertise as a trauma surgeon and a reserve tactical officer with the Dallas Police Department; Bruce Taylor, Ph.D., of the National Opinion Research Center and former PERF director of research, who discussed his research into the effects of ECW use on injuries to officers and subjects; Scott Greenwood of the American Civil Liberties Union, who provided the meeting participants with insight on policy based upon his work with several police agencies; and Doug Klint, president and general counsel of TASER International, Inc., who answered questions about his company's products.

We are especially grateful to those who participated in the working group the day after the executive session. This group spent a day working with PERF and COPS staffers to amend the 2005 guidelines and develop new ones, and then participated in several reviews of the draft guidelines. Members of the group included: Dr. Geoff Alpert, University of South Carolina; Brett Chapman, social science analyst at the National Institute of Justice; Alan Clarke, assistant commissioner of the New South Wales (Australia) Police Force; Dr. Alex Eastman, Dallas Police Department; Josh Ederheimer, then captain of the Washington, D.C., Metropolitan Police Department and now principal deputy director at the COPS Office; Mike Federico, staff superintendent of the Toronto Police Service; Mora Fiedler, senior social science analyst at the COPS Office; Mark Fisher, captain of the Philadelphia Police Department; John Gnagy, executive director of the National Tactical Officers Association; Fran Healy, lieutenant with the Philadelphia Police Department; Will Johnson, assistant chief of the Arlington (Texas) Police Department; Marc Joseph, deputy chief of the Las Vegas Metropolitan Police Department; Bill Lansdowne, chief of the San Diego Police Department; Robert Lehner, chief of the Elk Grove (California) Police Department; Marcus Martin, an officer of the Las Vegas Metropolitan Police Department; Charles McClelland, chief of the Houston Police Department; Ken Miller, deputy chief of the Charlotte-Mecklenburg Police Department; Kenton Rainey, chief of the Bay Area Rapid Transit Police Department; Tom Streicher, chief of the Cincinnati Police Department; Mark Warren, major of the Baltimore County Police Department; Jordan Watts, director of the Legal Bureau, Baltimore County Police Department; and Mick Williams, superintendent of the Victoria (Australia) Police.

Three individuals provided significant advice regarding the design of the project and the draft of this publication: Josh Ederheimer, Will Johnson, and Mark Warren. These leaders performed much of the original work on the 2005 CED guidelines when they worked at PERF and contributed their expertise to the effort to produce the new 2011 guidelines.

We also want to acknowledge Lorie Fridell, a professor at the University of South Florida, and Greg Meyer, retired captain of the Los Angeles Police Department, who provided advice that helped to produce better guidelines.

Finally, I would especially like to recognize the contributions of PERF staff who worked tirelessly on this project. Jerry Murphy, the project director, along with Molly Griswold and Debra Hoffmaster worked together to verse all aspects of the project, including the survey, the executive session, and this publication. Craig Fischer reviewed drafts and offered thoughtful editing. Bruce Kubu and Nate Ballard were invaluable to the survey process, providing support with the design and administration of the survey. Bill Tegeler helped with survey design and the drafting of guidelines. Kevin Greene helped to coordinate the conference and provide organizational assistance. PERF Fellow Jeff Egge (Minneapolis Police Department) uncovered critical information about ECWs and enthusiastically lent his experience as a police sergeant and planner to whatever project task needed his attention.

Chuck Wexler
Executive Director
Police Executive Research Forum

Introduction

In 2005, the Police Executive Research Forum (PERF), with support from the U.S. Department of Justice Office of Community Oriented Policing Services (COPS Office) produced a set of guidelines for the use of Conducted Energy Devices (CEDs). Many law enforcement agencies adopted the guidelines. In the years that followed, however, new information became available about how the weapons were being used, and controversy about CED safety continued. In 2010, PERF again received support from the COPS Office to revise the 2005 guidelines to reflect the most up-to-date knowledge regarding CED use and safety.

In the updated guidelines that follow, we changed the name of the weapons from CEDs to Electronic Control Weapons (ECWs) to reflect the reality that these tools are less-lethal weapons that are meant to help control persons who are actively resisting authority or acting aggressively.

ECWs are a popular tool among police and are increasingly being used in law enforcement agencies across the United States. Thousands of American police agencies have purchased ECWs for their officers, and industry representatives report that more than 15,500 law enforcement agencies in more than 40 countries are using ECWs (TASER 2010).

The rapid adoption and deployment of ECWs by law enforcement during the past five years have been accompanied by a number of benefits and controversy. Regarding the latter, a number of deaths have occurred proximate to the use of ECWs, resulting in concern about the limitations of the weapon. As a result, a significant amount of research has been conducted during the past several years by medical experts and other professionals to assess the injury risks associated with the use of ECWs. At the same time, police departments have reported that overall injury rates among suspects and officers have declined since they started using ECWs. In fact, PERF completed a study for the National Institute of Justice that found empirical support for those claims (Taylor et al. 2009).

Even among law enforcement agencies that adopted either the 2005 guidelines or similar policies that impose limits on the circumstances in which officers should use ECWs, some agencies are still considering whether they should further restrict their officers' use of these weapons in light of other developments. In 2009, TASER International, Inc., the leading manufacturer of ECWs, issued a training bulletin changing the recommended target area for ECWs away from the subject's chest. This advisory prompted police agencies to revisit their policy and training guidelines for ECW use. Court decisions also have caused agencies to continually review their policies, training, and oversight of ECWs to stay up-to-date with developments in the field.

The Project

The 2011 ECW guidelines are based on information gathered from interviews with police chiefs and other subject-matter experts, a 2010 PERF national survey of more than 190 law enforcement agencies that included questions about their use-of-force policies, and interviews with officials from a number of agencies that had experienced two or more deaths in the past five years that were considered "proximate to the use of an ECW." Most importantly, on August 3, 2010, PERF convened an executive session in Philadelphia that focused on ECW policy and practice. At that meeting, a cross section of 150 persons—police executives and practitioners of various ranks, authorities on use of force, medical doctors, attorneys, and researchers (see Appendix A)—discussed the findings of current ECW research, shared the experiences of police departments using ECWs, and identified additional challenges and issues for police executives as they maintain or consider the deployment of ECWs in their agencies.

On August 4, a working group of 25 executive session participants (see Appendix B)— including representatives of various ranks and positions in law enforcement agencies—spent a second day reviewing and modifying the 2005 guidelines, relying on the information presented at the previous day's conference and their considerable expertise with ECWs and use of force. Every effort was made to consider the views of all contributors and to incorporate the most up-to-date information and research findings. While the working group did not reach a unanimous recommendation for each guideline, in every instance it did achieve strong consensus and produced the new set of guidelines contained in this report. The new 2011 guidelines do not necessarily reflect the individual views of each participating law enforcement agency or the U.S. Department of Justice.

This report presents the revised guidelines, which represent the cumulative knowledge, experience, and expertise of police, medical, and legal professionals who shared their ideas and concerns. The Background Information section summarizes PERF's 2010 ECW survey results and highlights medical research and legal developments related to ECWs. A revised Glossary is also included.

Guiding Principles for ECWs

PERF recognizes that a large majority of police agencies have a successful history of ECW use, and the vast majority of law enforcement officers who use ECWs do so responsibly to resolve difficult situations. Without ECWs, many officers would have had to use a higher level of force, which might have increased suspect injuries and deaths. However, the use of ECWs in some instances has been controversial.

In general, the new guidelines in this report emphasize that ECWs are valuable and useful, but, like any weapon, they are not harmless, and the potential for injury can be exacerbated by inappropriate use and deployment of the devices. These guidelines are based on an understanding that the ECW is an essential part of an officer's toolbox in many police agencies.

The 2011 guidelines retain many of the original protocols from 2005, although there are some noteworthy differences. The substance of several guidelines has been changed, and there have been deletions, additions, and consolidations. The 2011 ECW guidelines are organized into six categories:

1. Agency Policy

2. Training

3. Using the ECW

4. Medical Considerations

5. Reporting and Accountability

6. Public Information and Community Relations

This information is meant to guide agencies as they consider how ECWs will be used in use-of-force scenarios. The guidelines are not standards or mandatory rules, and agencies should develop policies and training specific to their organizational needs. Agencies are encouraged to seek as much information as possible, including manufacturers' product warnings, when considering how and when to use ECWs.

The guidelines cannot anticipate every type of incident that officers may encounter. Law enforcement personnel must consider the rapidly changing dynamics of any situation, which is why the language of the guidelines is flexible. Agency personnel must always consider the totality of the circumstances when applying the guidelines. **In certain situations, exigent circumstances may outweigh the recommendation of a specific guideline. Personnel should always be able to articulate the justification for going outside of agency policy or training.**

Although law enforcement agencies have been using some variation of ECWs for more than 30 years, they are still a relatively new weapon for most officers. The number of agencies using them, and the number of ECWs in these agencies, has increased dramatically in just five years. As police agencies across the United States and in other nations gain more experience with ECWs, new information may alter how they use these weapons. The firsthand experiences of agencies, medical research, and legal developments may necessitate that PERF and other organizations again modify guidelines and model policies at some point in the future.

The 2011 guidelines are based on a set of principles that foster the responsible and accountable use of ECWs, while recognizing that they are an appropriate tool for officers who must resort to use of force. These guiding principles are the following:

1. ECWs should be considered less-lethal weapons.
2. ECWs should be used as a weapon of need, not a tool of convenience.
3. Officers should not over-rely on ECWs in situations where more effective and less risky alternatives are available.
4. ECWs are just one of a number of tools that police have available to do their jobs, and they should be considered one part of an agency's overall use-of-force policy.
5. In agencies that deploy ECWs, officers should receive comprehensive training on when and how to use ECWs.
6. Agencies should monitor their own use of ECWs and should conduct periodic analyses of practices and trends.
7. Agencies should consider the expectations of their community when developing an overall strategy for using ECWs.

Policy and Training Considerations

PERF believes that ECWs, when used appropriately and with a full understanding of their risks, are a useful weapon that can effectively help to resolve serious situations. ECWs can reduce the need for other force options and can enable officers to subdue actively resisting or aggressive subjects while lowering the rates of injury to law enforcement officers and subjects.

At the same time, ECWs are not harmless or risk-free, and ECWs should not be used in situations where alternative options, including other types of force or verbal de-escalation techniques, are more appropriate. Furthermore, ECWs do not always work as intended, so officers must be prepared to consider and exercise other force options when the ECW is not having its intended effect or continued use will endanger the subject.

ECWs are one of the newer force options for agencies to consider, and in all likelihood other weapons will become available in coming years. No weapon is a panacea for officers, and no weapon should be used at the expense of diminishing the fundamental skills of communicating with subjects and de-escalating tense encounters. When feasible, officers should use non-force options before using an ECW or other force options.

Agencies should not consider ECWs in isolation. Because ECWs and other force techniques and weapons have their own advantages and disadvantages, agencies should adopt a use-of-force policy that integrates ECWs with all other available force options to ensure officers contemplate all possibilities when considering any use of force. The comprehensive use-of-force policy should recognize that ECWs—as "less-lethal" and not "nonlethal" weapons—have the potential to result in a fatal outcome even when used in accordance with policy and training.

Risks Associated with ECWs

Knowledge of the effects of ECWs is changing rapidly as agencies gain experience with the weapons and as researchers examine their effects on officer and subject injuries. Police executives need to be aware of several factors relating to ECW technology and how ECWs are used by officers. The 2011 guidelines have been modified to reflect these factors, and the reasons for these particular new guidelines are explained here.

ECW Technology: Discontinuation of automatic cut-off feature may be problematic

Differences in the technology of particular ECW models can have policy implications. For example, the TASER X26® is different from some versions of the previous model, the TASER M26®. In early models of the M26, the activation cycle stopped at the five-second mark, while later models of the M26 and X26 can extend the activation for more than five seconds as long as the officer continually pulls the trigger. Both police executives and officers need to be aware of these differences, so that policy and training can incorporate these distinctions. At the 2010 meeting in Philadelphia, a number of police executives, based on first-hand experiences in their agencies, expressed concern that these differences may not be apparent to all officers, especially if they rarely use ECWs or transitioned from one model to another. As such, training for officers transitioning from earlier M26 versions to the more recent M26 or X26 model should emphasize that the newer model will continue to apply an electrical charge as long as the officer continues to depress the trigger.

Medical Considerations: Repeated or multiple applications may increase risk of death

It is important to recognize that ECWs have been cited by medical authorities as a cause of, or contributing factor in, some deaths.[1] A number of factors appear to be associated with fatal and other serious outcomes. These factors include how the ECW was used and the physical or medical condition of the subject who received an ECW application. Indeed, in July 2010 the American Academy of Emergency Medicine issued a Clinical Practice Statement advising physicians that they should consider additional evaluation and treatment for individuals who experienced an ECW application longer than 15 seconds (Vilke et al. 2010).

Although causation factors are not clear, the most common factors that appear to be associated with fatal and other serious outcomes include 1) repeated and multiple applications, 2) cycling time that exceeds 15 seconds in duration, whether the time is consecutive or cumulative, and 3) simultaneous applications by more than one ECW. **Officers must be trained to understand that repeated applications and continuous cycling of ECWs may increase the risk of death or serious injury and should be avoided.**

---

1   See Amnesty International 2008b, which details more than 35 such cases based on autopsy reports.

Medical Considerations: High-risk populations

Some populations currently believed to be at a heightened risk for serious injury or death following an ECW application include pregnant women, elderly persons, young children, visibly frail persons or persons with a slight build, persons with known heart conditions, persons in medical/mental crisis, and persons under the influence of drugs (prescription and illegal) or alcohol. Personnel should be trained about the medical complications that may occur after ECW use and should be made aware that certain individuals, such as those in a state of excited delirium, may be at a heightened risk for serious injury or death when subjected to ECW application or other uses of force to subdue them.

Medical Considerations: Positional asphyxia

Agencies also need to be cognizant of how positional asphyxia may exacerbate the condition of any individual who has received an ECW application. Positional asphyxia is a death that occurs when a subject's body position interferes with breathing, either when the chest is restricted from expanding properly or when the position of the subject's head obstructs the airway. Positional asphyxia has been mentioned as a possible contributing factor in a number of cases in which subjects died after one or more ECW applications. Police personnel should be trained to use a restraint technique that does not impair a subject's respiration following an ECW application.

Drive Stun: Avoid use as a pain-compliance tactic

The most commonly used ECWs can be used in two modes: probe and drive stun. Many police managers and officers erroneously believe that applications of drive stun are as effective as applications with probes, but that is not correct. The drive stun mode can be used to complete the circuit in the event that one of the probes is ineffective or becomes dislodged. The drive stun mode can also be used in close quarters for the purpose of protecting the officer or creating a safe distance between the officer and subject. Absent these circumstances, using the ECW in drive stun mode is of questionable value. The primary function of the drive stun mode, when not used to complete the circuit, is to gain subject compliance through the administration of pain. **Using the ECW to achieve pain compliance may have limited effectiveness and, when used repeatedly, may even exacerbate the situation by inducing rage in the subject.** For these reasons, agencies should carefully consider policy and training regarding when and how personnel use the drive stun mode, and should discourage its use as a pain compliance tactic. Drive stun has an applicable but limited purpose that should be taught, explained, and monitored during ECW training and field use.

Informed and Accountable Use of ECWs

Because ECWs are a relatively new weapon for most law enforcement officers, it is important for law enforcement agencies to continue to monitor and track how ECWs are used and maintain this comprehensive information to monitor agency-wide trends over time. This information should also be used to determine whether some officers are using ECWs more frequently or in a different manner than their fellow officers and if the uses are legitimate. Whenever possible, agencies should work collaboratively to collect and analyze information about ECW use to allow for comparisons across agencies. Furthermore, to evaluate ECWs as one element of a use-of-force strategy, law enforcement agencies ideally should gather such information for all force options.

When developing ECW policies, training, and deployment strategies, agencies should consult with one another to learn from each others' experiences. The U.S. Department of Justice has conducted research into ECWs, and those research reports may contain valuable information. In addition, police officials in Canada, the United Kingdom, and Australia may be able to provide guidance based on their experiences with ECWs. In the United Kingdom, for example, the Home Office and the Association of Chief Police Officers have done considerable work on ECWs. Agencies also should consider consulting with ECW manufacturers who may be able to provide technical information about their products. However, when an agency has questions about policy or training, or whether to implement or modify an ECW program, it should not rely solely on manufacturers for information.

To maintain good community engagement and support for law enforcement, agencies should involve community officials, leaders, and residents (including prosecutors, civil rights advocacy groups, medical professionals, mental health advocates, lawmakers, and interested community members) in the development of policy and accountability systems. After an ECW program is launched, these efforts should continue with community outreach programs to educate residents about ECWs, the reasons for adopting the weapons, their advantages and disadvantages when compared to other weapons, the risks posed by their use, how the agency intends to use them, and accountability systems that will be used to monitor use and collect information.

Conclusion

In a short time, ECWs have had a significant influence in American law enforcement agencies. Perhaps no other weapon has had such a dramatic impact. When used appropriately with a full understanding of their risks, ECWs are useful weapons that can effectively help officers to resolve serious situations. ECWs can reduce the need for more dangerous weapons and lower officer and subject injury rates, but they are not harmless and their usefulness has limitations. While the vast majority of police agencies have had tremendous success with the weapon, in some instances it appears that officers are using the ECW inappropriately or too frequently.

As more and more officers are armed with this weapon, police executives should ensure the responsible and accountable use of ECWs. The 2011 guidelines promote this goal, reflecting best practices and the recommendations of seasoned police officials, medical professionals, risk management authorities, and use-of-force experts. By considering the guidelines when developing agency policy and training, police agencies can promote the use of an effective law enforcement tool while minimizing the opportunity for negative outcomes.

The guidelines reflect what we learned in 2010. If the last five years are any indication, we can expect to see new research and laws that will shape policy guidelines in the future. It is vitally important that police agencies stay well informed of new developments that will help further refine use of this essential weapon.

Electronic Control Weapon Guidelines

Agency Policy

1. Agency personnel must always consider the totality of the circumstances when applying the guidelines. In certain situations, exigent circumstances may outweigh the recommendation of a specific guideline. Personnel should always be able to articulate the justification for going beyond agency policy or training.

2. Agencies should develop policies and training curricula for ECWs that are integrated with the agency's overall use-of-force policy.

3. Agencies should work to share and disseminate information regarding their respective ECW policies and training to foster better cooperation and coordination during joint law enforcement responses or operations. When possible, agencies should enter into a memorandum of understanding to develop joint ECW policies, protocols, and training.

4. Agencies should consult with local medical personnel to develop appropriate police-medical protocols for medical evaluation and removal of ECW probes following subjects' exposure to ECW application.

5. Agencies should consider adopting brightly colored ECWs (e.g., yellow), which may reduce the risk of escalating a force situation because they are plainly visible and thus decrease the possibility that a secondary unit will mistake the ECW for a firearm. (Note: Specialized units [e.g., SWAT units] may prefer dark-colored ECWs for tactical concealment purposes.)

6. Personnel should keep ECWs in a weak-side holster and should train to perform a weak-hand draw or cross-draw to reduce the possibility of accidentally drawing and/or firing a sidearm. Transitioning the ECW to the strong hand after drawing with the weak hand should be allowed.

7. If agencies permit personnel to use privately owned ECWs on duty, policy should dictate specifications, regulations, qualifications, etc. The privately owned ECWs should be registered with the agency.

Training

8. Before any agency personnel (e.g., officers, jail personnel, auxiliary/reserve officers, civilian staff) are armed with ECWs, they should receive all mandated training and achieve all qualification requirements.

9. Agencies should use scenario- and judgment-based training that recognizes the limitations of ECW application and the need for personnel to be prepared to transition to other force options as needed.

10. Agencies should not rely solely on training curriculum provided by an ECW manufacturer. When they do use the curriculum, agencies should ensure the manufacturer's training does not contradict agency use-of-force policies and values. Agencies should ensure that their ECW curricula are integrated into their overall use-of-force training curriculum.

11. Agencies should be aware that exposure to ECW application during training could result in injury to personnel and is not recommended. Any agency that does include ECW application as part of training should not make it mandatory for certification, and should ensure that safety protocols are rigorously followed.

12. ECW recertification should occur at least annually and should consist of physical competency and weapon retention, agency policy including any changes, technology changes, and reviews of local and national trends in ECW use. Recertification should also include scenario-based training.

13. Personnel should be trained to use an ECW for one standard cycle (five seconds) and then evaluate the situation to determine if subsequent cycles are necessary. Training protocols should emphasize that multiple applications or continuous cycling of an ECW resulting in an exposure longer than 15 seconds (whether continuous or cumulative) may increase the risk of serious injury or death and should be avoided.

14. Training protocols should emphasize the risk of positional asphyxia, and thus officers should be trained to use a restraint technique that does not impair the subject's respiration following an ECW application.

15. Personnel should be trained that when a subject is armed with an ECW and attacks or threatens to attack a police officer who is alone, the officer must defend himself or herself or take actions to avoid becoming incapacitated and risking the possibility that the subject could gain control of the officer's firearm. However, if multiple officers are present, a subject's attack with an ECW against one officer should not in and of itself cause a deadly-force response by other officers.

16. Agencies' policy and training should discourage the use of the drive stun mode as a pain compliance technique. The drive stun mode should be used only to supplement the probe mode to complete the incapacitation circuit, or as a countermeasure to gain separation between officers and the subject so that officers can consider another force option.

17. Personnel should be trained to attempt hands-on control tactics during ECW application, including handcuffing the subject during ECW application (i.e., handcuffing under power). Training should emphasize that personnel who touch a subject during ECW application will not receive exposure to the electrical charge, so long as caution is taken not to touch the subject along the circuit (i.e., between the locations of the two probes).

18. Command staff, supervisors, and investigators should receive ECW awareness training appropriate to the investigations they conduct and review.

19. If an agency uses more than one model of ECWs, training should emphasize the differences in the various models (e.g., duration of cycle, optimal probe spread).

20. In addition to providing an overview of ECWs, agencies should provide ECW awareness training to personnel who are not certified to carry the devices and emphasize their responsibilities. The training should also cover situations such as attempting to handcuff subjects during ECW application and transitioning to other force options.

Using the ECW

21. Personnel should use an ECW for one standard cycle (five seconds) and then evaluate the situation to determine if subsequent cycles are necessary. Personnel should consider that exposure to the ECW for longer than 15 seconds (whether due to multiple applications or continuous cycling) may increase the risk of death or serious injury. Any subsequent applications should be independently justifiable, and the risks should be weighed against other force options.

22. A warning should be given to a subject prior to activating the ECW unless doing so would place any person at risk. Warnings may be in the form of verbalization, display, laser painting, arcing, or a combination of these tactics.

23. When feasible, an announcement should be made to other personnel on the scene that an ECW is going to be activated.

24. Personnel should not intentionally activate more than one ECW at a time against a subject.

25. ECWs should be used only against subjects who are exhibiting active aggression or who are actively resisting in a manner that, in the officer's judgment, is likely to result in injuries to themselves or others. ECWs should not be used against a passive subject.

26. Fleeing should not be the sole justification for using an ECW against a subject. Personnel should consider the severity of the offense, the subject's threat level to others, and the risk of serious injury to the subject before deciding to use an ECW on a fleeing subject.

27. ECWs should not generally be used against pregnant women, elderly persons, young children, and visibly frail persons. Personnel should evaluate whether the use of the ECW is reasonable, based upon all circumstances, including the subject's age and physical condition. In some cases, other control techniques may be more appropriate as determined by the subject's threat level to others.

28. Personnel should not intentionally target sensitive areas (e.g., head, neck, genitalia).

29. ECWs should not be used on handcuffed subjects unless doing so is necessary to prevent them from causing serious bodily harm to themselves or others and if lesser attempts of control have been ineffective.

30. ECWs should not be used against subjects in physical control of a vehicle in motion (e.g., automobiles, trucks, motorcycles, ATVs, bicycles, scooters).

31. ECWs should not be used when a subject is in an elevated position where a fall may cause substantial injury or death.

32. ECWs should not be used in the known presence of combustible vapors and liquids or other flammable substances including alcohol-based Oleoresin Capsicum (O.C.) spray carriers. Agencies utilizing both ECWs and O.C. spray should use a non-combustible (e.g., water-based) spray.

33. ECWs can be effective against aggressive animals. Policies should indicate whether use against animals is permitted.

Medical Considerations

34. Personnel should be aware that there is a higher risk of sudden death in subjects under the influence of drugs and/or exhibiting symptoms associated with excited delirium.

35. When possible, emergency medical personnel should be notified when officers respond to calls for service in which they anticipate an ECW application may be used against a subject.

36. All subjects who have been exposed to ECW application should receive a medical evaluation by emergency medical responders in the field or at a medical facility. Subjects who have been exposed to prolonged application (i.e., more than 15 seconds) should be transported to an emergency department for evaluation. Personnel conducting the medical evaluation should be made aware that the suspect has experienced ECW activation, so they can better evaluate the need for further medical treatment.

37. All subjects who have received an ECW application should be monitored regularly while in police custody even if they received medical care. Documentation of the ECW exposure should accompany the subject when transferred to jail personnel or until the subject is released from police custody.

38. ECW probes should be treated as a biohazard. Personnel should not remove ECW probes from a subject that have penetrated the skin unless they have been trained to do so. Only medical personnel should remove probes that have penetrated a subject's sensitive areas or are difficult to remove.

Reporting and Accountability

39. ECWs should be regulated while personnel are off duty under rules similar to those for service firearms (including storage, transportation, use, etc.).

40. A supervisor should respond to all incident scenes where an ECW was activated.

41. When possible, supervisors should anticipate on-scene officers' use of ECWs and should respond to calls for service that have a high propensity for the use of an ECW.

42. A supervisor should conduct an initial review of each ECW activation, and every instance of ECW use, including unintentional activation, should be documented.

43. Agencies should initiate force investigations when any of the following factors is involved:

    — A subject experiences a proximity death or serious injury following ECW application

    — A subject experiences prolonged ECW application (longer than 15 seconds)

    — The ECW appears to have been used in a punitive or abusive manner

    — There appears to be a substantial deviation from ECW training or policy

    — A subject in an at-risk category has been subjected to application (e.g., young children, individuals who are elderly/frail, pregnant women, and any other activation as determined by a supervisor)

44. Every ECW-related enhanced force investigation (and when possible every preliminary investigation) should include:

    — Interviews of the subject and all officers who discharged their ECWs

    — Location and interviews of witnesses (including other officers)

    — Forensic quality photographs (including a ruler to show distances) of subject and officer injuries

    — Photographs of cartridges/probes

    — Collection of ECW cartridges, probes, data downloads, car video, confetti tags

    — Copies of the ECW data download

    — Other information as indicated in Reporting and Accountability Guideline #50

45. When reviewing downloaded ECW data, supervisors and investigators should be aware that the total time of activation registered on an ECW may not reflect the actual duration of ECW application on a subject.

46. ECW activations should be tracked in the agency's early intervention system (EIS).

47. Agencies should periodically conduct random audits of ECW data downloads and reconcile use-of-force reports with recorded activations. Agencies should take necessary action as appropriate when inconsistencies are detected.

48. Audits should be conducted to verify that all personnel who carry ECWs have attended initial and recertification training.

49. Agencies should collect and analyze information to identify ECW trends. Agencies may include display, laser painting, and arcing of weapons to measure prevention/deterrence effectiveness. Agencies should periodically analyze ECW statistics and make them available to the public.

50. Agencies should collect the following information about ECW use:

    — Date, time, location of incident

    — The use of display, laser painting and/or arcing, and whether those tactics deterred a subject and gained compliance

    — Identifying and descriptive information and investigative statements of the subject (including membership in an at-risk population), all personnel firing ECWs, and all witnesses

    — The type and brand of ECW used

    — The number of ECW activations, the duration of each cycle, the duration between activations, and (as best as can be determined) the duration that the subject received applications

    — Level of aggression encountered

    — Any weapons possessed by the subject

    — The type of crime/incident the subject was involved in

    — Determination of whether deadly force would have been justified

    — The type of clothing worn by the subject

— The range at which the ECW was used

— The type of mode used (probe deployment or drive stun)

— The point of probe impact on a subject with the device in probe mode

— The point of impact on a subject with the device in drive stun mode

— Location of missed probe(s)

— Terrain and weather conditions during ECW use

— Lighting conditions

— The type of cartridge used

— Suspicion that subject was under the influence of drugs (specify if available)

— Medical care provided to the subject

— Any injuries incurred by personnel or the subject

Public Information and Community Relations

51. Law enforcement agencies should conduct neighborhood programs that focus on ECW awareness training, which should be part of any citizen's training academy program.

52. Agencies' public information officers should receive extensive training on ECWs so they can better inform the media and the public about the weapon. Members of the media should be briefed on agencies' policies and use of ECWs.

53. ECW awareness should extend to law enforcement partners such as local medical personnel, citizen review boards, medical examiners, mental health professionals, judges, and local prosecutors.

Background Information

PERF's 2010 Survey: What Is the State of the Field Regarding ECW Use?

To gather information about current policy, practice, and training on ECWs, PERF conducted a survey of its member law enforcement agencies as well as an additional 50 agencies (n=346) that were surveyed during the 2005 project to develop the original guidelines. A total of 194 (56%) agencies from the United States and Canada responded, representing cities, counties, states, and a few smaller municipalities. The survey was conducted during a four-week period in the summer of 2010. Highlights of the survey results are presented below.

The majority of the responding agencies (90%) were using ECWs and, to be more specific, one of several models developed by TASER International, Inc.[2] The number of ECWs in agencies ranged from a low of two to a high of 4,479. ECWs were being carried by patrol officers, supervisors, traffic officers, detectives, SWAT officers, school resource and crisis intervention officers, and civilian employees. In most agencies, ECWs were assigned to individual officers, while a smaller number of agencies distributed ECWs to officers at the beginning of a shift.

Activation Rate

In 2009, the number of ECW activations in responding law enforcement agencies ranged from 0 to 473.[3] The ECW activation rate (the number of activations per ECW per year) ranged from 0 to 3.18, with a median activation of 0.25 and a mean of 0.38.

As illustrated by the chart on the right, the majority of reporting agencies had relatively low activation rates, which averaged less than once a year per ECW.

Activations Per ECW (2009)	
▶ 0 to 0.19 activations	63 agencies
▶ 0.2 to 0.39 activations	45 agencies
▶ 0.4 to 0.59 activations	27 agencies
▶ 0.6 to 0.79 activations	7 agencies
▶ 0.8 to 0.99 activations	2 agencies
▶ > 1 activation	10 agencies
▶ > 2 activations	2 agencies
▶ > 3 activations	1 agency

---

2   Of the agencies using ECWs, 90% reported using the TASER X26 model.

3   157 agencies of the 194 were able to provide the number of activations recorded in 2009.

Written Policy and Procedure

Approximately half of the agencies that responded to the PERF survey included their ECW policy as part of their use-of-force policy, while slightly fewer than half had a separate or stand-alone policy.

The placement of ECWs on the use-of-force continuum varied somewhat among agencies.[4] Most placed ECWs in the intermediate range on the continuum, either equal to or just below chemical incapacitants, chemical/kinetic hybrids, and strikes/batons. Only a few agencies had ECWs directly beneath deadly force. At the low end of the force spectrum, only a few agencies had ECWs equal to control holds. A significant majority allowed the ECW to be used when officers encountered active resistance (80%) or aggressive resistance (91%). A much lower number of agencies (7%) allowed the use of an ECW when an officer encountered passive resistance—a use that the 2005 guidelines recommended against, as do the new 2011 guidelines contained in this report.

We asked participating agencies whether their written policy provided guidance in a variety of circumstances that officers might encounter in their interactions with suspects or other persons. Overall, there was significant variation in the extent to which agencies provided guidance.

For example, in situations involving persons with a mental, physical, or developmental disability, slightly fewer than half of reporting agencies indicated that their written policy discouraged the use of ECWs against these persons. In circumstances involving an elderly person or a juvenile, a person under the influence of drugs or alcohol, or a person threatening suicide, closer to two-thirds of the agencies indicated that their written policy provided guidance that strongly discouraged the use of an ECW on these individuals except in exigent circumstances.

The circumstance that was addressed most often in written policy pertained to the use of an ECW on a handcuffed subject. Seventy-one percent of agencies strongly discouraged the use of ECWs against a handcuffed subject except in situations where the subject was acting aggressively or to prevent injury to the subject, the officer, or others.

In situations where deadly force is appropriate, most agencies indicated that the use of the less-lethal ECW is at the discretion of the officer.

---

4   A number of agencies indicated that they were no longer using the use-of-force continuum.

Agencies reported that they used or consulted a variety of resources in the development of their policies. The most frequently cited external resources were the ECW manufacturer and professional law enforcement organizations. Medical professionals, prosecutors, political leaders, and citizen groups were consulted less often.

Training

All agencies that responded to the survey required officers to be certified before they could use ECWs. However, the number of hours of training required for certification varied widely—from 2 to 40 hours, with 8 hours the block of time most often reported. The majority of agencies required recertification, and most of those required recertification annually.

We also asked about the practice, employed by some law enforcement agencies but not recommended by the guidelines, of requiring exposure to an ECW during training. Fewer than one-fourth of the agencies required exposure, but more than half permitted exposure on a voluntary basis. Officer injuries as a result of such ECW activations were reported by 13% of the agencies.

The majority of agencies used an ECW curriculum that was a combination of law enforcement agency and manufacturer training, and most agencies covered similar topics in their training, including excited delirium, de-escalation techniques, crisis intervention, and recognition of medical or mental illness or disability.

The survey also found that most agencies were specific about how the ECW must be carried, and the majority required officers to carry the ECW on their weak side.

Activating the ECW

Most agencies do not specify the maximum number of cycles that an officer can administer during an interaction with a subject, nor do those agencies specify the duration of each cycle. However, of those agencies that do provide such guidance in their written policy, the maximum number of cycles is three and the duration of each cycle is five seconds.

The most frequently recommended target areas when using the weapon in the probe mode are the back and lower body; in the drive stun mode, it is the lower body, extremities, and the back.

Accountability and Reporting

The survey included a number of questions to assess what occurs after an ECW is used against a subject. Medical care is generally required after an application, including response by fire service or EMS personnel to the scene and/or a physician assessment at a hospital/medical facility. After an application, most agencies require officers to complete some type of report. The survey results indicated that 91% of agencies require a use-of-force report and 31% require a specialized ECW report. Approximately 70% of reporting agencies require a supervisor to respond to the scene, and 97% routinely require a supervisor to review the application. A variety of evidence is collected after an application, including photographs of suspect injuries; downloading of data from the ECW; and collection of patrol car videos, probes/darts, and the confetti tags that eject from an ECW to facilitate identification of which cartridge was used at a specific location. Most agencies conduct annual analyses of ECW applications, and most conduct ECW inspections and data audits.

What Is the Medical Evidence Regarding the Effects of ECWs?

Initially, the ECW was introduced to law enforcement as a low-risk device that could be used as a substitute for lethal force and save lives. This less-lethal tool would allow officers to control unruly subjects and minimize injuries to offenders and officers. While there is considerable evidence that deployment of ECWs is associated with reductions in officer and offender injuries (Taylor et al. 2009), adverse effects related to the use of ECWs have also been documented, including injuries from the probes and injuries from falls.

In addition, the debate involving deaths following the use of ECWs continues to generate concern among law enforcement officials and the public. From June 2001 to August 31, 2008, 351 persons in the United States died after being subjected to ECW activations by police, according to Amnesty International USA (2008a). "In most cases coroners have attributed the deaths to other causes, such as drug intoxication or 'excited delirium,'" Amnesty International said. "However, in at least 50 cases, coroners are reported to have listed the Taser as a cause or contributory factor in the death." The human rights group said "safety research to date has not answered the question of what role Taser shocks may be playing in these deaths" but expressed concern that ECWs are being used excessively "as tools of routine force" (Amnesty International 2008b).

TASER International, the leading manufacturer of ECWs, vigorously disputed the numbers and conclusions of Amnesty International. TASER International maintains that, although a relative few medical examiners have implicated ECWs as a contributory factor in deaths following an ECW application, many other factors were present and that the true cause of many of those deaths was excited delirium (PR Newswire 2004). TASER International has frequently said that TASERS do not cause cardiac arrest and reiterated this point in a 2009 training bulletin, which stated, "While it may not be possible to say that an [ECW] could never affect the heart under any circumstances, the risk of VF (ventricular fibrillation) is extremely rare and would be rounded to near zero." TASER International also pointed to animal research suggesting that ECWs have virtually no risk for healthy human beings (Valentino et al. 2008). Moreover, TASER International claimed that its products have prevented injuries and saved many lives by providing police officers with an alternative to deadly force (Sunnucks and O'Grady 2008).

During the past five years, a substantial amount of medical research has been conducted to understand the effects of ECWs. According to remarks delivered by Dr. Alexander Eastman[5] at PERF's 2010 executive session, approximately 145 scientific papers are available in the medical literature on this topic, and nearly half of those were published fairly recently, since November 2007. These papers encompass a wide range of research methodologies, including case studies, opinion papers, and reviews and studies with both human and animal test populations. Only a few studies document actual field use of ECWs.

Recent ECW Studies and Findings

The following provides an overview of the most relevant and substantive studies and the findings that contribute to our current understanding of the effects of ECWs.

One of the most common concerns raised about the use of ECWs is the cardiac effect of the electrical charge that is transmitted by the weapon. According to Dr. Eastman's review of the existing medical literature, there has never been a documented cardiac effect on humans under actual use in laboratory research studies. However, research scientists have been able to simulate a cardiac effect in swine (Valentino et al. 2008). The correlation of those results in animals to humans is unknown.

---

5   Alexander Eastman is the Deputy Medical Director for the Dallas Police Department and an Assistant Professor of Surgery at the University of Texas, Southwestern Medical Center.

At least one independent study looked at the cardiac effect of the TASER X26 and its relationship to delayed or sudden cardiac arrest in normal adults. The study found that "it is highly unlikely that the TASER X26 can cause ventricular fibrillation minutes to hours after its use through direct cardiac effects of the electric field generated by the TASER" (Ideker and Dosdall 2007).

Other studies have considered other underlying medical conditions that were identified in individuals who died subsequent to the use of an ECW. In a study using methamphetamine-intoxicated sheep as the test population, there was no incidence of ventricular fibrillation after the animal was subjected to an ECW application (Dawes et al. 2010).

Other researchers have looked at the physiologic effects of the ECW on individuals after exercise and on intoxicated individuals. Using adult subjects and healthy volunteers, these studies did not report any adverse physiologic reactions in the test subjects (Vilke et al. 2009; Moscati et al. 2010).

Real-World ECW Application Studies

One of the major considerations in reviewing the medical literature is that much of the existing work is laboratory-based and not necessarily reflective of conditions in the field. The following are summaries of recent studies of "real-world" applications of ECWs during actual use-of-force incidents.

A 15-month study of police activations of ECWs was conducted in 2004 in a large U.S. city to examine police compliance with policies regarding proper ECW use and to track any associated medical events following ECW applications. Researchers documented 426 applications during the study period and recorded one death, attributed to lethal toxic hyperthermia. The study concluded that by using ECWs, officers avoided the use of lethal force in a significant number of instances (Eastman et al. 2008).

A 2008 study funded by the National Institute of Justice examined ECW use by law enforcement officers during interaction with suspects. Six law enforcement agencies participated in the study, which included a mandatory physician review of police and medical records following every ECW activation against a subject. During a 36-month period, approximately 1,200 incidents were reviewed. The study reported that "more than 99% of subjects do not experience significant injuries after conducted electrical weapon use. Two subjects died in police custody but medical examiners did not find ECW use to be causal or contributory in either case" (Bozeman et al. 2009).

In 2009, Dr. Jared Strote at the University of Washington Medical Center examined the medical records of nearly 900 persons who were subjects of an ECW activation by the Seattle Police Department over a six-year period. According to the study, "less than one percent required hospital admission for an injury related to the restraint (i.e., ECW) incident. No deaths occurred, even when patients exhibited signs of excited delirium" (Strote et al. 2010).

According to a report released by the National Institute of Justice (2008), "There is no conclusive medical evidence within the state of current research that indicates a high risk of serious injury or death from the direct effects of [ECW] exposure. Field experience with [ECW] use indicates that exposure is safe in the vast majority of cases." Those findings are based on a medical panel mortality review of ECW deaths and the panel's review of currently available medical research.

In July 2010, the American Academy of Emergency Medicine issued a Clinical Practice Statement advising physicians to consider additional evaluation and treatment for individuals who experienced an ECW application longer than 15 seconds (Vilke et al. 2010). This evidence-based medical advisory indicates that ECW applications longer than 15 seconds may have effects on the human body that could contribute to serious injury or death. The advisory also reflects the anecdotal experiences of many agencies that have had ECW proximity deaths. In many of these instances, the subject received an ECW activation, either continuously or cumulatively, of longer than 15 seconds.[6]

---

6   Telephone and in-person interviews with police agency representatives conducted by PERF staff, June 15–July 28, 2010.

What Are the Legal Considerations Associated with ECWs?

As with other litigation involving allegations of excessive force by law enforcement, courts consider police use of ECWs under the standards set by the U.S. Supreme Court in *Graham v. Connor*.[7] In that landmark 1989 ruling, the Court held that citizens' claims of excessive force should be reviewed using the 4th Amendment "objective reasonableness" standard and "from the perspective of a reasonable officer on the scene, rather than with 20/20 vision of hindsight."[8] The Court said that "the calculus of reasonableness must embody allowance for the fact that police officers are often forced to make split-second judgments—in circumstances that are tense, uncertain, and rapidly evolving—about the amount of force that is necessary in a particular situation."[9]

Case law specific to ECWs is currently developing, and there is little precedent in some jurisdictions. Police departments need to remain aware of pertinent cases not only in their own jurisdictions but also across the country. As case law develops, courts are looking to one another for guidance on ECW issues. As part of our research, PERF reviewed a number of U.S. Court of Appeals cases relevant to ECWs. These recent cases addressed issues such as ECW use on a restrained subject, on subjects suspected of a minor offense, and on a woman known to be pregnant.

Recent Cases in the Ninth Circuit

Two of the most closely watched and potentially far-reaching ECW cases in recent years have been in the U.S. Court of Appeals for the Ninth Circuit. The first of these cases came from the Southern District of California. In *Bryan v. MacPherson*[10], an officer stopped plaintiff Carl Bryan for driving without a seatbelt. Bryan, who had already been pulled over for speeding earlier in the day, was agitated and stepped out of the vehicle wearing only his boxer shorts and tennis shoes. It was undisputed that Bryan was "yelling gibberish and hitting his thighs" but did not verbally threaten the officer, who was standing 20 feet away. Bryan did not attempt to flee, but the officer saw him take a step toward him. Without warning, the officer activated his ECW and Bryan fell to the ground, suffering facial contusions and fracturing four teeth.

---

7   490 U.S.386 (1989).

8   Id. at 396.

9   Id. at 396-397.

10   608 F.3d 614 and No. 08-55622 (9th Cir. 2010).

In its opinion, the Ninth Circuit reviewed a number of other cases and studies by medical professionals and law enforcement research groups that analyzed the nature and quality of an intrusion when an ECW is used against a subject. The Court noted:

> We recognize the important role controlled electric devices like the Taser
> X26 can play in law enforcement. The ability to defuse a dangerous situation
> from a distance can obviate the need for more severe, or even deadly, force
> and thus can help protect police officers, bystanders, and suspects alike. We
> hold only that the X26 and similar devices when used in dart-mode constitute
> an intermediate, significant level of force that must be justified by the
> governmental interest involved.[11]

The panel of judges in the Ninth Circuit found that Bryan's behavior, though erratic, was nonviolent and he was unarmed. The Court also found that the officer's use of the ECW was excessive, as Bryan did not pose an immediate threat to anyone, including the officer. "An unarmed, stationary individual, facing away from an officer at a distance of fifteen to twenty-five feet, is far from an 'immediate threat' to that officer," the Court said.[12]

Although the Court found that the use of the ECW against Bryan was not reasonable, the officer was granted qualified immunity in this matter because there was little case law when the incident occurred (2005) to support the belief that the TASER X26 in probe mode would constitute an intermediate level of force. Since then, however, a number of changes in the case law support the ECW as an intermediate level of force. Though the Ninth Circuit recently refused to rehear the case *en banc* to reconsider the immunity issue, today the Ninth Circuit would likely rule differently on the question of officer immunity.

The second Ninth Circuit case of interest came from the District Court for the Western District of Washington. In *Brooks v. City of Seattle*, plaintiff Malaika Brooks was issued a notice of infraction for speeding, and she repeatedly refused the officer's demand that she sign the notice.[13] When ordered from her vehicle, even when shown the officer's ECW, Brooks refused to do so and informed officers at the scene that she was pregnant. One officer took the keys out of the ignition and another used his ECW to drive stun Brooks on the

---

11   No. 08-55622 at 18918 (9th Cir. 2010).

12   Id. at 18920.

13   599 F.3d 1018 (9th Cir. 2010).

arm, thigh, shoulder, and neck. After each stun, Brooks honked her horn and started to yell. Officers eventually removed Brooks from the vehicle and handcuffed her.

In its initial 2–1 decision, a three-member panel in the Ninth Circuit found that the use of the drive stun was not excessive force and that it constituted a "less-than-immediate use of force, prefaced by warnings and other attempts to obtain compliance, against a suspect accused of a minor crime, but actively resisting arrest, out of police control, and posing some slight threat to officers."[14] On September 30, 2010, the Ninth Circuit agreed to hear the case *en banc* (by all nonrecused judges on the court), noting that the three-judge panel opinion shall not be cited as precedent by, or to, any court of the Ninth Circuit.[15] Police agencies should be aware of this impending decision and its potential implications on how courts view the use of the drive stun.

Level of Offense

Several other circuits have reviewed the use of ECWs on subjects in light of the severity of their suspected crimes and the potential threat they pose to officers. In *Brown v. City of Golden Valley*, plaintiff Sandra Brown's husband was stopped when officers suspected him of driving while intoxicated and she was a passenger in the vehicle.[16] The Eighth Circuit found that "it was unreasonable to, without warning, taser a nonviolent passenger who was not fleeing or resisting arrest and was suspected of a minor, nonviolent crime, because she had disobeyed two orders to get off the telephone with a 9-1-1 operator."[17] In this 2009 decision, the Court noted that "[t]he Taser is a relatively new implement of force, and case law related to the Taser is developing."[18]

Also in 2009, the Eleventh Circuit decided the case of *Oliver v. Fiorino*, where Anthony Oliver appeared to be mentally unstable when officers observed him standing in the median of a major road, claiming that people were shooting at him.[19] Although initially compliant with the officers, Oliver began to walk into traffic. An officer discharged her ECW against

---

14   Id.

15   No. 08-35526 (9th Cir. 2010), available at www.ca9.uscourts.gov/datastore/opinions/2010/10/05/08-35526o.pdf

16   547 F.3d 491 (8th Cir. 2009).

17   Id.

18   Id. at 495.

19   586 F.3d 898 (11th Cir. 2009).

Oliver at that time, and she testified that she continued "pulling the trigger until he stayed on the ground," cycling it between 8 and 12 times, during which time officers did not attempt to restrain Oliver. Oliver died later at the hospital and, according to the Court, "[h]is body temperature rose to 107 degrees and he ultimately died as a result of the Taser shocks."[20]

In its decision, the Eleventh Circuit pointed out that "no decision from the United States Supreme Court, or from this Court, or from the Florida Supreme Court, has clearly established that an officer's repeated use of a Taser constituted excessive force under circumstances like these."[21] Even so, the Court considered that Oliver did not pose an immediate threat to officers or others, nor was he suspected of any crime, and concluded that "the force employed was so utterly disproportionate to the level of force reasonably necessary that any reasonable officer would have recognized that his actions were unlawful."[22]

The Tenth Circuit also ruled in 2007 that the use of an ECW on an individual who was suspected of a minor offense, and who was not threatening or fleeing, was unreasonable. In *Casey v. City of Federal Heights*[23], Edward Casey removed his own traffic court file from the courthouse while he went outside to retrieve money to pay his fine. As Casey walked back into the courthouse, the officer attempted to stop him. Casey continued to walk, and the officer tackled him, placing him in an arm-lock and jumping on Casey's back. Additional officers arrived, and without warning Casey was subjected to ECW activation and a drive stun. Officers also "repeatedly banged his face into the concrete," the Court noted. The Court refused to grant qualified immunity, and the case was remanded to the District Court for a determination on the Constitutionality of the use of force.[24]

In contrast to the above decisions, the Ninth Circuit in 2010 found it was reasonable to use an ECW on a domestic violence victim who was not suspected of a serious crime but who exacerbated a tense situation. In *Mattos v. Agarano*[25], officers responded to a domestic disturbance at the Mattos home. Jayzel Mattos put her hands up when the officer arresting her husband bumped into her. Upset that she had touched him, the officer used his ECW against

---

20   Id. at 906.
21   Id. at 907.
22   Id. at 908.
23   509 F.3d 1278 (10th Cir. 2007).
24   Id.
25   590 F.3d 1082 (9th Cir. 2010).

Mattos for one cycle, and she was arrested for obstructing government operations. The Court found that although Mattos's actions did not constitute a serious crime, the officer's use of the ECW was reasonable because her actions "exacerbated an already tense and rapidly escalating situation" where the officers "had an important interest in obtaining immediate control."[26]

Use of ECWs on Restrained Subjects

Other cases have looked at the use of ECWs on restrained individuals. In 2007, the Sixth Circuit found that ECW use on a restrained, but not handcuffed, subject was "unnecessary and gratuitous."[27] In that case, the plaintiff fled from officers during a domestic incident investigation; following the pursuit, he was restrained by one officer while another repeatedly used her ECW on him.[28]

However, the Eleventh Circuit found in two recent cases that ECW use on handcuffed subjects was not excessive when the subjects continued to resist. In a 2009 case, an ECW was used on a suspect who was actively resisting while she was in handcuffs and leg shackles. In *Mann v. TASER International, et al*[29], Melinda Fairbanks had been smoking methamphetamine and refused to leave a neighbor's home. Even after being placed into handcuffs and leg shackles, Fairbanks violently resisted, kicking out a patrol car window and banging her head on the car. The Court found that the ECW use against Fairbanks was not excessive, as Fairbanks was violent and aggressive "and the evidence demonstrates that she was clearly a danger to herself and others."[30] Fairbanks died later that day from malignant hyperthermia, with a body temperature of 107 degrees; the Court found insufficient evidence to hold that the ECW was the cause of her death.[31]

---

26 Id. at 1088-1089.

27 Roberts v. Mangold, 240 Fed. Appx. 675 (6th Cir. 2007).

28 Id.

29 No. 08-16951 (11th Cir. 2009).

30 Id.

31 Id.

In 2008, the Eleventh Circuit found that ECW use was not excessive when used against a suspect who resisted by refusing to stand and walk to a patrol car. In that case, *Buckley v. Haddock*[32], Jesse Buckley was stopped for speeding and was arrested when he refused to sign the ticket. While handcuffed, Buckley sat down and refused to walk to the officer's vehicle, and the officer applied his ECW three times in drive stun against Buckley. The Eleventh Circuit cited three key factors in making its decision:

1. The incident occurred on a dark highway with considerable traffic.

2. Buckley was resisting.

3. The officer took several steps to gain compliance prior to applying the ECW.

Although Buckley was handcuffed, the court found that he was not "fully secured" and that the officer's "gradual use of force, culminating with his repeated (but limited) use of a taser [...] was not unconstitutionally excessive."[33]

TASER Training Bulletin 15.0

In October 2009, TASER International released "Training Bulletin 15.0 Regarding Medical Research Update and Revised Warnings," which offered a new preferred target zone for ECWs. It lowered the recommended target area from "center of mass" to "lower center of mass" for front shots. By avoiding the chest whenever possible, TASER International indicated that law enforcement agencies may avoid the "controversy about whether [ECWs] do or do not affect the human heart."[34]

The new recommendation created confusion in the law enforcement community and heightened concerns about police agencies' liability. Some law enforcement officials have said they do not understand why the bulletin was issued, given the manufacturer's assertion that the weapon, when used properly, is safe. TASER International contends that the change is not a new policy and that the recommendation is based on risk management principles, not medical or safety concerns (2009).

---

32   No. 07-10988 (11th Cir. 2008).

33   Id.

34   Id.

Many police agencies across the country changed their policies and training to follow the new instructions to aim at "lower center of mass." PERF's survey asked whether agencies were aware of the bulletin and whether they had made changes to their training or written policy in response to the new information. All of the responding agencies indicated that they were aware of the bulletin. As a result, approximately 90% indicated that changes were made to their ECW certification training, and half of the agencies made changes to their written policy.

References

Amnesty International. 2008a. "List of Deaths Following Use of Stun Weapons in U.S. Law Enforcement: June 2001 to 31 August 2008." London: Amnesty International Publications. www.amnestyusa.org/uploads/ListOfDeaths.pdf

Amnesty International. 2008b. *"Less than Lethal"? The Use of Stun Weapons in U.S. Law Enforcement*, 61–74. London: Amnesty International Publications. www.amnesty.org/en/library/asset/AMR51/010/2008/en/530be6d6-437e-4c77-851b-9e581197ccf6/amr510102008en.pdf

Bozeman, W., W. E. Hauda, J. J. Heck, et al. 2009. "Safety and Injury Profile of Conducted Electrical Weapons Used by Law Enforcement Officers against Criminal Suspects." *Annals of Emergency Medicine* 53:480–489.

Dawes, Donald M., Jeffrey D. Ho, Jon B. Cole, et al. 2010. "Effect of Electronic Control Device Exposure on a Methamphetamine-Intoxicated Animal Model. *Academic Emergency Medicine* 17:436–443.

Eastman, A. L., J. C. Metzger, P. E. Pepe, et al. 2008. "Conductive Electrical Devices: A Prospective, Population-Based Study of the Medical Safety of Law Enforcement Use." *Journal of Trauma* 64:1567–72.

Ideker, Raymond E., and Derek J. Dosdall. 2007. "Can the Direct Cardiac Effect of the Electric Pulses Generated by the TASER X26 Cause Immediate or Delayed Sudden Cardiac Arrest in Normal Adults?" *American Journal of Forensic Medical Pathology* 28:195–201.

Moscati, Ronald, Jeffrey D. Ho, Donald M. Dawes, and James R. Miner. 2010. "Physiologic Effects of Prolonged Conducted Electrical Weapon Discharge in Ethanol-Intoxicated Adults." *American Journal of Emergency Medicine* 28:582–587.

National Institute of Justice. 2008. *Study of Deaths Following Electro Muscular Disruption: Interim Report.* Washington, D.C.: National Institute of Justice. www.ncjrs.gov/pdffiles1/nij/222981.pdf

PR Newswire. 2004. "TASER International, Inc. Demands Amnesty International Withdraw Its Misleading and Defamatory Statements." News release (June 2). www.prnewswire.com/news-releases/taser-international-inc-demands-amnesty-international-withdraw-its-misleading-and-defamatory-statements-74306762.html

Strote, J., M. Walsh, M. Angelidis, A. Basta, and H. R. Hutson. 2010. "Conducted Electrical Weapon Use by Law Enforcement: An Evaluation of Safety and Injury." *Journal of Trauma* 68:1239–46.

Sunnucks, Mike, and Patrick O'Grady. 2008. "Amnesty International Calls for Moratorium on Tasers, Other Stun Guns." *Phoenix Business Journal* (December 16). www.bizjournals.com/phoenix/stories/2008/12/15/daily24.html

TASER International, Inc. 2010 "TASER Technology." Press Kit. www.taser.com/company/pressroom/Documents/Press%20Kit%2012%2005%2010.pdf

———. 2009. "TASER Training Bulletin 15.0 Regarding Medical Research Update and Revised Warnings." Memorandum to law enforcement agencies (October 16). www.ecdlaw.info/outlines/10-15-09%20TASER%20ECD%20Trng%20Memo%20w%20Trng%20Bulletin%20and%20Warnings.pdf

Taylor, Bruce, et al. 2009. *Comparing Safety Outcomes in Police Use-of-Force Cases for Law Enforcement Agencies That Have Deployed Conducted Energy Devices and a Matched Comparison Group That Have Not: A Quasi-Experimental Evaluation.* Report submitted to the National Institute of Justice. Washington, D.C.: Police Executive Research Forum. http://meetings.policeforum.org/upload/CED%20outcomes_193971463_10232009143958.pdf

Valentino, D. J., et al. 2008. "TASER X26 Discharges in Swine: Ventricular Rhythm Capture is Dependent on Discharge Vector." *Journal of Trauma* 65:1478–1487.

Vilke, Gary M., Theodore C. Chan, and William P. Bozeman. 2010. "What Evaluations Are Needed in Emergency Department Patients after a TASER Device Activation?" Clinical Practice Statement. American Academy of Emergency Medicine (July 12). www.aaem.org/emtopics/taser_evaluations.pdf

Vilke, G. M., C. M. Sloane, A. Suffecool, et al. 2009. "Physiologic Effects of the Taser After Exercise." *Academy of Emergency Medicine* 8:771–773.

Glossary

activation. Pulling the trigger of an ECW, causing arcing or probe discharge.

active aggression. A threat or overt act of an assault (through physical or verbal means), coupled with the present ability to carry out the threat or assault, which reasonably indicates that an assault or injury to any person is imminent.

active resistance. A subject's physical actions to defeat an officer's attempt at control and to avoid being taken into custody. Verbal statements alone do not constitute active resistance.

Anti-Felon Identification (AFID) tags. See **confetti tags**.

application. The actual contact and delivery of electrical impulse to the subject via probe discharge or drive stun.

arcing. Pulling the trigger to activate an ECW without discharging the probes. This may be done as a warning to the subject or to test the ECW prior to deployment (sometimes referred to as a spark test).

cartridge. A replaceable vessel that generally contains compressed gas, probes, connecting wires, and confetti tags.

complete the circuit. When there is not adequate spread between probes attached to a subject, or one probe misses the subject or dislodges, the ECW may be used in drive stun mode to incapacitate the subject. This allows for the electrical pulse to travel between the attached probe(s) and the point where the front of the ECW makes contact with the subject. This tactic is sometimes referred to as a three-point contact.

Conducted Energy Device (CED). See **Electronic Control Weapon (ECW)**.

confetti tags. Small identifying cards expelled from an ECW cartridge when probes are discharged. Each confetti tag contains a serial number unique to the specific cartridge used. Confetti tags are sometimes referred to as Anti-Felon Identification (AFID) tags.

cycle. The period during which electrical impulses are emitted from the ECW following activation. In most models, a standard cycle is 5 seconds for each activation. The duration of a cycle may be shortened by turning the ECW off but may be extended in certain models by continuing to pull the trigger.

display. Drawing and exhibiting the ECW as part of a warning tactic, typically accompanied by appropriate verbalization.

drive stun. Drive stun mode is possible whether or not the cartridge has been expended or removed from the ECW. (If the cartridge is not removed, the probes will enter the body.) This action requires pulling the trigger and placing the ECW in direct contact with the subject, causing the electric energy to enter the subject directly. Drive stun is frequently used as a non-incapacitating pain compliance technique. It may also be used to incapacitate the subject where at least one probe is attached to the subject's body and the ECW contact will complete the circuit.

duration. The aggregate time that the ECW is activated. It is important to note that the duration of activation may differ from the duration of time that a subject is subjected to the electrical impulse from the ECW.

Electronic Control Weapon (ECW). A weapon designed primarily to discharge electrical charges into a subject that will cause involuntary muscle contractions and override the subject's voluntary motor responses. Originally called Conducted Energy Device (CED).

excited delirium. State of extreme mental and physiological excitement, characterized by behaviors and symptoms such as extreme agitation, elevated body temperature (hyperthermia), watering eyes (epiphoria), hostility, exceptional strength, and endurance without fatigue.

exigent circumstances. Circumstances that would cause a reasonable person to believe that prompt and unusual action is necessary to prevent physical injury to self or others.

firing. Discharging ECW probes at an intended target.

fleeing. An active attempt by a person to avoid apprehension by a law enforcement officer through evasive actions while attempting to leave the scene.

laser painting. The act of unholstering and pointing an ECW at a subject and activating the ECW's laser dot to show that the weapon is aimed at the subject.

less-lethal weapon. Any apprehension or restraint tool that, when used as designed and intended, is less likely to cause death or serious injury than a conventional police lethal weapon (e.g., firearm).

neuromuscular incapacitation. The effect of the ECW on a subject when, through the application of an electrical pulse, the ECW dominates the motor nervous system by interfering with electrical signals sent to the skeletal muscles by the central nervous system.

passive resistance. Physical actions that do not prevent the officer's attempt to control, for example, a person who remains in a limp-prone position, passive demonstrators, etc.

positional asphyxia. Death that occurs when a subject's body position interferes with breathing, either when the chest is restricted from expanding properly or when the position of the subject's head obstructs the airway.

probe discharge. Pulling the trigger to release the probes from the cartridge to make contact with the subject and achieve neuromuscular incapacitation.

probe spread. The amount of distance between probes fired from an ECW.

probes. Projectiles with wires contained in an ECW cartridge. When the ECW is discharged, probes are expelled from the ECW and penetrate the subject's clothing and/or skin, allowing application of the electric impulse.

proximity death. The death of a subject following exposure to an ECW.

sensitive areas. An area of the subject's body that may cause more serious injury to the subject if struck with an ECW probe (e.g., head, neck, genitalia)

serious bodily harm. An injury to a person that, either at the time of the actual injury or at a later time, involves a substantial risk of death, serious permanent disfigurement, or protracted loss or impairment of any part or organ of the body, as well as any breaks, fractures, or burns of the third degree.

three-point contact. See **complete the circuit.**

Appendix A: PERF Executive Session Participants[35]

Philadelphia, PA, August 3, 2010

Deputy Chief Hassan Aden
Alexandria (Virginia) Police Department

Professor Geoff Alpert
University of South Carolina

Mr. Joseph P. Aviola, Jr.
Wilmington University

Staff Inspector Jerrold Bates
Philadelphia Police Department

Executive Director Christina Beamund
Atlanta Citizen Review Board

Superintendent Stephen Beckett
Waterloo Regional Police Service (Canada)

Captain John L. Bell, Jr.
Virginia Beach Police Department

Mr. Andrew Bellwoar
Siana, Bellwoar & McAndrew, LLP

Deputy Chief Merritt Bender
Howard County (Maryland) Police
Department

Assistant Attorney General Sharon Benzil
Maryland Transportation Authority Police

Sergeant Scott Berning
Fort Wayne (Indiana) Police Department

Deputy Commissioner Kevin Bethel
Philadelphia Police Department

Deputy Chief Michael Blakely
Riverside (California) Police Department

Assistant Chief William Bochter
Pittsburgh Police Department

Sergeant Robert K. Boehm
Providence (Rhode Island) Police
Department

Litigation Counsel Michael A. Brave
TASER International, Inc.

Deputy City Attorney James Brown
City Attorney's Office, Riverside, California

Chief Kenneth M. Burton
Columbia (Missouri) Police Department

Sergeant Rickey Butler
Tuscaloosa (Alabama) County Sheriff's
Office

Police Commissioner Patrick Carroll
New Rochelle (New York) Police
Department

Senior Scientist Joseph J. Cecconi
National Institute Of Justice

Chief Teresa C. Chambers
Riverdale Park (Maryland) Police
Department

Social Science Analyst Brett Chapman
National Institute of Justice

---

35   All information reflects the capacity in which attendees participated in the 2010 executive session.

Chief Michael Chitwood
Daytona Beach (Florida) Police Department

Deputy Chief Legal Counsel Thea G. Clark
Hillsborough County (Florida) Sheriff's
Office

Assistant Commissioner Alan Clarke
New South Wales Police Force (Australia)

Chief Inspector William Colarulo
Philadelphia Police Department

Assistant Chief Mike Crosbie
Prince William County (Virginia) Police
Department

Dr. Donald Dawes, M.D.
EmCare, Santa Barbara, California

Professor Albert DiGiacomo
West Chester University of Pennsylvania

Chief Kim C. Dine
Frederick (Maryland) Police Department

Assistant Chief Neil Dryfe
Hartford (Connecticut) Police Department

Lieutenant Henry Dugan
Philadelphia Police Department

Dr. Alexander L. Eastman, MD
Dallas Police Department

Sergeant Charles Ebner
Philadelphia Police Department

Captain Josh Ederheimer
Washington, D.C. Metropolitan Police
Department

Chief Dean M. Esserman
Providence (Rhode Island) Police
Department

Sergeant Fred Farris
Lenexa (Kansas) Police Department

Staff Superintendent Michael Federico
Toronto Police Service (Canada)

Senior Social Science Analyst Mora Fiedler
Office of Community Oriented Policing
Services

Captain Mark Fisher
Philadelphia Police Department

Deputy Commissioner William Flanagan
Nassau County (New York) Police
Department

Associate Professor Lorie Fridell
University of South Florida

Deputy Commissioner John J. Gaittens
Philadelphia Police Department

Acting Assistant Chief Paul Galligan
Norfolk (Virginia) Police Department

Deputy Chief Scott Gerlicher
Minneapolis Police Department

Executive Director John Gnagy
National Tactical Officers Association

Deputy Chief Vincent Golbeck
Dallas Police Department

Captain Alan Goldberg
Montgomery County (Maryland) Police
Department

Research Coordinator Kevin E. Greene
Police Executive Research Forum

Attorney Scott Greenwood
American Civil Liberties Union, Cincinnati

Captain Alec Griffin
Richmond (Virginia) Police Department

Research Associate Molly Griswold
Police Executive Research Forum

Director of Training Rudy Grubesky
Pennsylvania Municipal Police Officers'
Education and Training Commission

Major Ronald Hartman
Springfield (Missouri) Police Department

Deputy Chief James Hawthorne
Arlington (Texas) Police Department

Lieutenant Francis Healy
Philadelphia Police Department

Staff Lieutenant Ashley Heiberger
Bethlehem (Pennsylvania) Police
Department

Senior Assistant Sergeant at Arms Michael Heidingsfield
United States Senate Sergeant at Arms

Chief William M. Heim
Reading (Pennsylvania) Police Department

Deputy Chief Bruce Herridge
York Regional Police (Canada)

Mr. Terry G. Hillard
Hillard Heintze, Chicago, Illinois

Senior Associate Debra Hoffmaster
Police Executive Research Forum

Mr. Peter Holran
TASER International, Inc.

Dr. Richard Hourgh
University of West Florida

Captain Harmon W. Hunsicker
Metro Nashville Police Department

Assistant Chief Will Johnson
Arlington (Texas) Police Department

Chief James W. Johnson
Baltimore County Police Department

Deputy Chief Marc Joseph
Las Vegas Metropolitan Police Department

Chief Administrative Officer Nola Joyce
Philadelphia Police Department

President & Counsel Doug Klint
TASER International, Inc.

Attorney Karen Kruger
Maryland Chiefs of Police Association

Lieutenant Edward Lang
Philadelphia Police Department

Captain Jay Lanham
Prince William County (Virginia) Police
Department

Chief William Lansdowne
San Diego Police Department

Mr. Chris W. Lawrence
Ontario Police College (Canada)

Lieutenant Roland Lee
Philadelphia Police Department

Chief Timothy Lee
Dartmouth (Massachusetts) Police
Department

Chief Robert M. Lehner
Elk Grove (California) Police Department

Captain Theresa Levins
Philadelphia Police Department

Chief Inspector Richard Lewis
Association of Chief Police Officers (UK)

Major Roger A. Lewis
Kansas City (Missouri) Police Department

National President Edwin Maldonado
National Latino Peace Officers Association

Police Officer Marcus Martin
Las Vegas Metropolitan Police Department

Lieutenant Joseph Maum
Philadelphia Police Department

Lieutenant Carl Maupin
Leesburg (Virginia) Police Department

Professor R. Paul McCauley
Indiana University of Pennsylvania

Chief Charles A. McClelland, Jr.
Houston Police Department

Sergeant Calvin McGee
New Rochelle (New York) Police
Department

Chief William J. McMahon
Howard County (Maryland) Police
Department

Director Bernard Melekian
Office of Community Oriented Policing
Services

Captain Greg Meyer (Ret.)
Los Angeles Police Department

Deputy Chief Ken Miller
Charlotte-Mecklenburg (North Carolina)
Police Department

Chief Ronald Miller
Topeka (Kansas) Police Department

Assistant Chief Joseph A. Moore
Newport News (Virginia) Police Department

Professor Francis R. Murphy
Ramapo College, New Jersey

Director Gerard Murphy
Police Executive Research Forum

Chief Richard Myers
Colorado Springs Police Department

Commander Stephen Mylett
Corpus Christi (Texas) Police Department

Commander Robert Osborne
Los Angeles County Sheriff's Department

Research Assistant Stephanie Pratt
National Institute Of Justice

Executive Director William O'Toole
Northern Virginia Training Academy

Chief Jason Parker
Dalton (Georgia) Police Department

Chief Kenton W. Rainey
Bay Area Rapid Transit (California) Police
Department

Commissioner Charles Ramsey
Philadelphia Police Department

Captain Patrick Redding
New Haven (Connecticut) Police
Department

Mr. Charles D. Reynolds
Police Performance Solutions, LLC

Deputy Chief Cy Ritter
Kansas City (Missouri) Police Department

Chief Tony Ross
United States Marshals Service

Assistant Director Ronald Ruecker
Federal Bureau of Investigation

Captain Dennis M. Santos
Virginia Beach Police Department

Chief Doug Scott
Arlington (Virginia) Police Department

Sergeant Joseph M. Seitz
Milwaukee (Wisconsin) Police Department

Senior Social Science Analyst Amy Schapiro
Office of Community Oriented Policing
Services

Lieutenant John Shelton
Durham (North Carolina) Police
Department

Captain Kenneth J. Shultz
High Point (North Carolina) Police
Department

Lieutenant Thomas Sims
San Jose Police Department

Chief of Detectives Steven Skyrnecki
Nassau County (New York) Police
Department

Lieutenant Mark A. Smith
University of Texas at Houston Police
Department

Attorney Robert Spence
Tuscaloosa County (Alabama) Sheriff's
Office

Chief Deputy Rebecca Spiess
Mesa County (Colorado) Sheriff's Office

Chief Thomas Streicher
Cincinnati Police Department

Assistant Chief Morris Tabak
San Francisco Police Department

Lieutenant Thomas Taffe
New York Police Department

Principal Research Scientist Bruce Taylor
National Opinion Research Center

Chief Ronald Teachman
New Bedford (Massachusetts) Police
Department

Deputy Director William Tegeler
Police Executive Research Forum

Officer Luke Tedstone
Sherborn (Massachusetts) Police Department

Chief Richard Thompson, III
Sherborn (Massachusetts) Police Department

Assistant Chief Drew Tracy
Montgomery County (Maryland) Police
Department

Captain Shawn Trush
Philadelphia Police Department

Captain Thomas Verdi
Providence (Rhode Island) Police
Department

Lieutenant Bob Wagner
Howard County (Maryland) Police
Department

Deputy Chief Benjamin Walton
Daytona Beach (Florida) Police Department

Major Mark Warren
Baltimore County Police Department

Director Penny Westfall
Iowa Law Enforcement Academy

Executive Director Chuck Wexler
Police Executive Research Forum

Chief James E. Williams
Staunton (Virginia) Police Department

Superintendent Mick Williams
Victoria Police (Australia)

Chief Jon Zumalt
North Charleston (South Carolina) Police
Department

Appendix B: Working Group Participants[36]

Philadelphia, PA, August 4, 2010

Dr. Geoff Alpert
University of South Carolina

Social Science Analyst Brett Chapman
National Institute of Justice

Assistant Commissioner Alan Clarke
New South Wales Police Force (Australia)

Dr. Alex Eastman
Dallas Police Department

Captain Josh Ederheimer
Washington, D.C. Metropolitan Police Dept.

Staff Superintendent Mike Federico
Toronto Police Service (Australia)

Senior Social Science Analyst Mora Fiedler
Office of Community Oriented Policing
Services

Captain Mark Fisher
Philadelphia Police Department

Executive Director John Gnagy
National Tactical Officers Association

Lieutenant Francis Healy
Philadelphia Police Department

Assistant Chief Will Johnson
Arlington (Texas) Police Department

Deputy Chief Marc Joseph
Las Vegas Metropolitan Police Department

Chief Bill Lansdowne
San Diego Police Department

Chief Robert Lehner
Elk Grove (California) Police Department

Officer Marcus Martin
Las Vegas Metropolitan Police Department

Chief Charles McClelland
Houston Police Department

Deputy Chief Ken Miller
Charlotte-Mecklenburg (North Carolina)
Police Department

Chief Kenton Rainey
Bay Area Rapid Transit (California) Police
Department

Chief Tom Streicher
Cincinnati Police Department

Major Mark Warren
Baltimore County Police Department

Legal Bureau Director Jordan Watts
Baltimore County Police Department

Superintendent Mick Williams
Victoria Police (Australia)

---

36   All information reflects the capacity in which attendees participated in the 2010 working group.

PERF Staff

Chuck Wexler, Executive Director

Jerry Murphy, Director

Bill Tegeler, Deputy Director

Debra Hoffmaster, Sr. Research Associate

Molly Griswold, Research Associate

Kevin Greene, Research Coordinator

Sergeant Jeff Egge, PERF Fellow
Minneapolis Police Department

About the COPS Office

THE OFFICE OF COMMUNITY ORIENTED POLICING SERVICES (THE COPS OFFICE) is the component of the U.S. Department of Justice responsible for advancing the practice of community policing by the nation's state, local, and tribal law enforcement agencies through information and grant resources. The community policing philosophy promotes organizational strategies that support the systematic use of partnerships and problem-solving techniques to proactively address the immediate conditions that give rise to public safety issues such as crime, social disorder, and fear of crime. In its simplest form, community policing is about building relationships and solving problems.

The COPS Office awards grants to state, local, and tribal law enforcement agencies to hire and train community policing professionals, acquire and deploy cutting-edge crime-fighting technologies, and develop and test innovative policing strategies. The COPS Office funding also provides training and technical assistance to community members and local government leaders and all levels of law enforcement.

Since 1994, the COPS Office has invested more than $16 billion to add community policing officers to the nation's streets, enhance crime fighting technology, support crime prevention initiatives, and provide training and technical assistance to help advance community policing. More than 500,000 law enforcement personnel, community members, and government leaders have been trained through COPS Office-funded training organizations.

The COPS Office has produced more than 1,000 information products—and distributed more than 2 million publications—including Problem Oriented Policing Guides, Grant Owners Manuals, fact sheets, best practices, and curricula. And in 2010, the COPS Office participated in 45 law enforcement and public-safety conferences in 25 states in order to maximize the exposure and distribution of these knowledge products. More than 500 of those products, along with other products covering a wide area of community policing topics—from school and campus safety to gang violence—are currently available, at no cost, through its online Resource Information Center at www.cops.usdoj.gov. More than 2 million copies have been downloaded in FY2010 alone. The easy to navigate and up to date website is also the grant application portal, providing access to online application forms.

About PERF

FOUNDED IN 1976, THE POLICE EXECUTIVE RESEARCH FORUM (PERF) IS A POLICE
research organization and a provider of high-quality management services, technical assistance,
and executive-level education to support law enforcement and the criminal justice system.
As a private, nonprofit organization, PERF was formed to improve the delivery of police
services through:

▶ The exercise of strong national leadership

▶ Public debate of police and criminal justice issues

▶ Research and policy development

▶ The provision of vital management and leadership services to police agencies

PERF's founding principles include improving police service by continuing to professionalize police
executive management; fostering research, growth, and knowledge of police science and administration;
and supporting the continuing development and implementation of standards to improve police
performance. PERF has an extensive history of measuring all aspects of police agency performance,
striving to find the best policing practices, and disseminating that knowledge to police agencies.

PERF conducts innovative police and criminal justice research and provides a wide variety of
management and technical assistance programs to police agencies throughout the world. PERF's
groundbreaking projects on community and problem-oriented policing, racial profiling, use-of-force
issues, and crime reduction strategies have earned it a prominent position in the police community.

PERF also works toward increased professionalism and excellence in the field through its training
and publications programs. PERF sponsors and conducts the Senior Management Institute for Police
(SMIP), which provides comprehensive professional management and executive development training
to police chiefs and law enforcement executives. Convened annually in Boston, SMIP offers instruction
by professors from leading universities, including many from Harvard University's Kennedy School of
Government, as well as by leading police practitioners.

PERF has also developed and published some of the leading literature in the law enforcement field, including the following:

It's More Complex Than You Think: A Chief's Guide to DNA (2010)

Guns and Crime: Breaking New Ground By Focusing on the Local Impact (2010)

Gang Violence: The Police Role in Developing Community-Wide Solutions (2010)

Violent Crime and the Economic Crisis: Police Chiefs Face a New Challenge, Parts I & II (2009)

The Stop Snitching Phenomenon: Breaking the Code of Silence (2009)

Violent Crime in America: What We Know About Hot Spots Enforcement (2008)

Police Chiefs and Sheriffs Speak Out On Local Immigration Enforcement (2008)

Promoting Effective Homicide Investigations (2007)

Violent Crime in America: "A Tale of Two Cities" (2007)

Police Planning for an Influenza Pandemic: Case Studies and Recommendations from the Field (2007)

Patrol-Level Response to a Suicide Bomb Threat: Guidelines for Consideration (2007)

Strategies for Resolving Conflict and Minimizing Use of Force (2007)

"Good to Great" Policing: Application of Business Management Principles in the Public Sector (2007)

A Gathering Storm: Violent Crime in America (2006)

Police Management of Mass Demonstrations: Identifying Issues and Successful Approaches (2006)

Strategies for Intervening with Officers through Early Intervention Systems: A Guide for Front-Line Supervisors (2006)

Conducted Energy Devices: Development of Standards for Consistency and Guidance (2006)

Issues in IT: A Reader for the Busy Police Chief Executive (2005)

Supervision and Intervention within Early Intervention Systems: A Guide for Law Enforcement Chief Executives (2005)

Managing a Multi-Jurisdiction Case: Identifying Lessons Learned from the Sniper Investigation (2004)

Patrol Training Officer (PTO) Program (2004)

Community Policing: The Past, Present and Future (2004)

Recognizing Value in Policing: The Challenge of Measuring Police Performance (2002)

Racially Biased Policing: A Principled Response (2001)

Citizen Involvement: How Community Factors Affect Progressive Policing (2000)

Problem-Oriented Policing: Crime-Specific Problems, Critical Issues and Making POP Work (3 volumes, 1998–2000)

To learn more about PERF, visit www.policeforum.org

The **2011 Electronic Control Weapon Guidelines** publication is based on information gathered from workshops, interviews, and a national survey that examined the use of ECWs. In August 2010, an executive session comprising police, medical, and legal professionals convened in Philadelphia to focus on ECW policy and practice. Afterward, a concentrated working group spent a second day reviewing and modifying an earlier set of guidelines produced in 2005. As a result, this 2011 revised version represents the collective knowledge, experience, and expertise of participants who shared their ideas and concerns throughout this process. This publication is intended to guide law enforcement agencies as they consider how ECWs can be used in use-of-force situations, balancing responsibility and accountability as well as recognizing that ECWs are appropriate weapons when officers must resort to use of force.

www.ingramcontent.com/pod-product-compliance
Lightning Source LLC
Chambersburg PA
CBHW081613170526
45166CB00009B/2948